GEGE AKUTAMI

I yelled out, "Please give me more compliments!" But no one did. I guess that's because I was the only one at the office...

GEGE AKUTAMI published a few short works before starting *Jujutsu Kaisen*, which began serialization in *Weekly Shonen Jump* in 2018.

JUJUTSU KAISEN

VOLUME 2
SHONEN JUMP MANGA EDITION

BY GEGE AKUTAMI

TRANSLATION Stefan Koza
TOUCH-UP ART & LETTERING Snir Aharon
DESIGN Shawn Carrico
EDITOR John Bae
CONSULTING EDITOR Erika Onabe

Printed in Italy

Published by VIZ Media, LLC
P.O. Box 77010
San Francisco, CA 94107

10 9 8
First printing, February 2020
Eighth printing, December 2021

viz.com

JUJUTSU KAISEN

2

FEARSOME WOMB

STORY AND ART BY GEGE AKUTAMI

—CURSE—

Hardship, regret, shame... The misery that comes from these negative human emotions can lead to death.

Yuji Itadori is an athletically gifted student who doesn't care much about school. However, one fateful day, he finds himself protecting his school from a Curse by swallowing the severed finger of the legendary demon Ryomen Sukuna! Side by side with the Jujutsu Sorcerer Megumi Fushiguro, they manage to defeat the threat.

Now that Itadori houses the soul of Sukuna, the most infamous curse in human history—his fate is sealed with a death sentence. But Itadori receives an unexpected stay of execution under one condition—Itadori will be allowed to live until he's collected and consumed all remaining pieces of Sukuna, so that when he's executed Sukuna will be eliminated as well. Under these unusual circumstances, Itadori now finds himself enrolled at Jujutsu High.

Jujutsu High
First-Year
Megumi Fushiguro
Jujutsu High
First-Year
Nobara Kugisaki
Special Grade
Jujutsu Sorcerer
Satoru Gojo
Jujutsu High
Assistant Manager
Kiyotaka Ijichi

JUJUTSU KAISEN

2

FEARSOME WOMB

CHAPTER 8 Fearsome Womb, Part 3 7

CHAPTER 9 Fearsome Womb, Part 4 27

CHAPTER 10 After the Rain 47

CHAPTER 11 A Dream 67

CHAPTER 12 Pushing Forward 87

CHAPTER 13 Watching Movies 107

CHAPTER 14 Assault 127

CHAPTER 15 Domain 147

CHAPTER 16 Affection 167

CHAPTER 8:
FEARSOME WOMB,
PART 3

WITHOUT A DOUBT ...
...YOU'RE SUCH AN ANNOYING BRAT!
PAT PAT
GAH
HOLD ON...
I'M THINKING.
IF I GO AFTER FUSHIGURO, THE KID WILL CHANGE BACK. AND IF THAT'S THE CASE, THEN THE MOST TROUBLESOME SITUATION FOR HIM WOULD BE...

VS
THIS! IT'S BACK TO THE ORIGINAL PLAN.
KSH
HEY.
LET'S GO KILL THE BRATS.
BLOP
COME ON!
BA DUM
BA DUM
BA DUM
BADUM
KREEE

YOU FOOL!
VOOM
GUAAH!
BLP
BLOP

BOFF
OOPS!
I FIXED THIS TOO.
NOT A FAN OF WALKS, HUH?
WELL, I GUESS CURSES ARE SUPPOSED TO LINGER AT THEIR POINT OF ORIGIN.
FINE, THEN...
YOU CAN DIE HERE!

WHAM
C'MON...
YOU CAN DO BETTER THAN THAT!

KRAK
CRASH
SHD
SWF
HUH?

SHNK
!!!
EVEN A CURSED SPIRIT...
...NEEDS AN ARM, RIGHT?

HEH...
HEH...
HEH HEH...
HAHAHAHAHAHAHA
PLEASE EXPAND THE EVACUATION ZONE TO TEN KILOMETERS.
WHAT ABOUT YOU, FUSHI-GURO?
I'M STAYING.

IF THINGS GO WRONG...
...IT'S MY RESPONSIBILITY TO FINISH HIM.
BUT I DON'T WANT TO LET HIM DIE!
YES, IT'S A PERSONAL OPINION. PLEASE DO SOMETHING ABOUT IT.
AFTER I TAKE KUGISAKI TO THE HOSPITAL...
...I'LL BE BACK AS SOON AS I CAN.
NO.
YOU WON'T MAKE MUCH OF A DIFFERENCE ANYWAY.
STAB
IF YOU DO COME BACK, PLEASE BRING A GRADE 1 OR STRONGER JUJUTSU SORCERER.
THERE'S PROBABLY NO ONE AVAILABLE THOUGH.
DID YOU KNOW? YOU AND I ARE CATEGORIZED AS SPECIAL GRADE.
ME...

AND THIS INSECT?
HAHHH HAHHH
GUH...
GLP
GLP GLP GLP GLP

SPLASH
HEH
YOU LOOK PROUD OF YOURSELF—SHOULD I APPLAUD?
BUT USING CURSED ENERGY TO HEAL YOURSELF ISN'T HARD FOR CURSED SPIRITS, UNLIKE HUMANS.
YOU AND THIS BRAT...
...DON'T HAVE THE SLIGHTEST IDEA OF WHAT A CURSE CAN DO.
HOW ABOUT...
...I TEACH YA...
SPLISH
...TRUE JUJUTSU SORCERY ?!
SHF

DOMAIN EXPANSION...
MALEVOLENT SHRINE

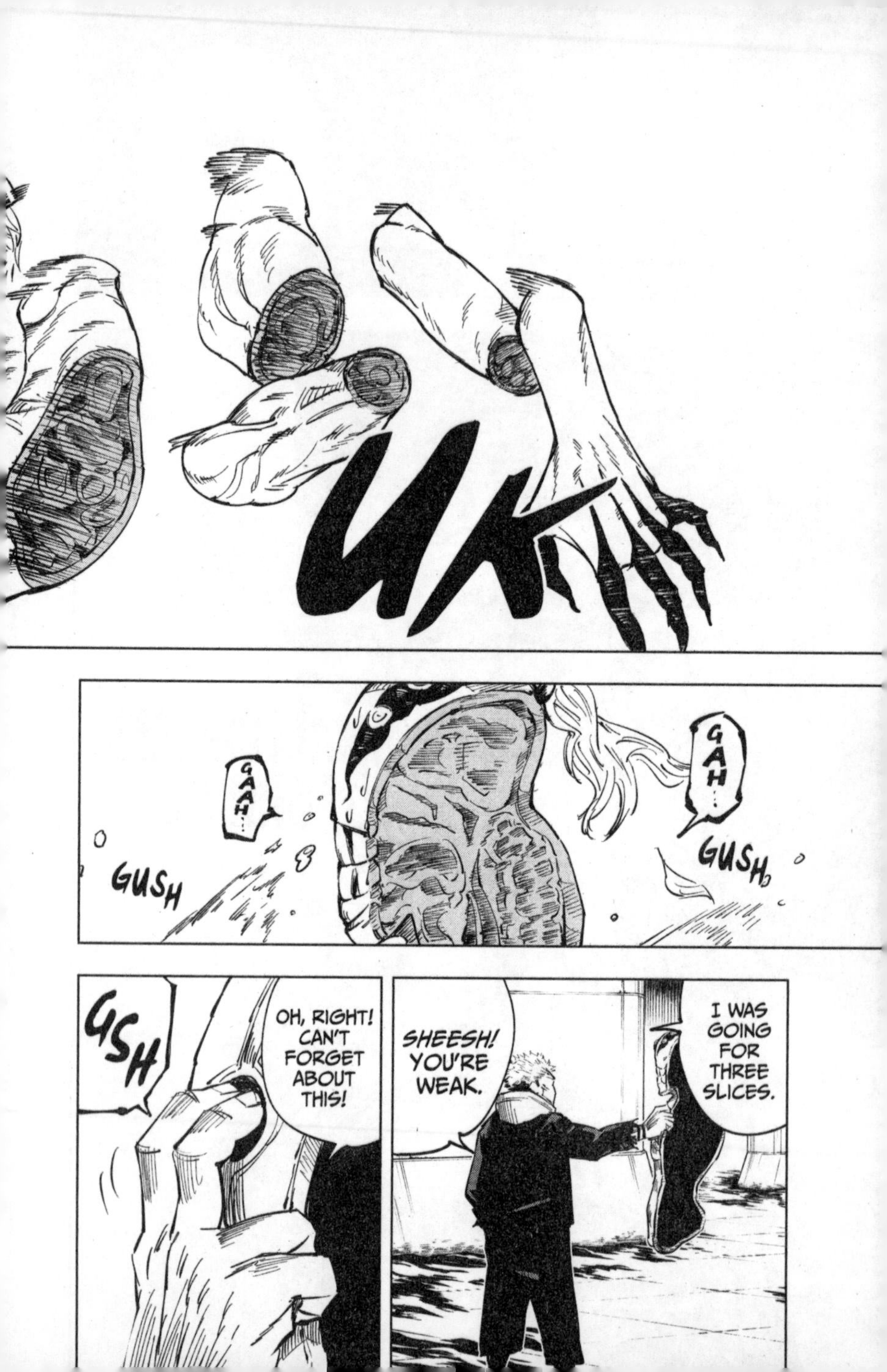
UK
GAH...
GAAH...
GUSH
GUSH
I WAS GOING FOR THREE SLICES.
SHEESH! YOU'RE WEAK.
OH, RIGHT! CAN'T FORGET ABOUT THIS!
GSH

SH
FWP
I'LL TAKE THAT BACK.
GUSH
GUSH
GUSH

BOOF
I'M DONE!
HOW ANNOYING! IF YOU'RE GOING TO CHANGE, GET ON WITH IT ALREADY ...
...BRAT?
...

!!
THE DOMAIN IS GONE!!
THE SPECIAL GRADE IS DEAD!
NOW WE WAIT FOR ITADORI TO COME BACK...
HE AIN'T COMING BACK.
IT SEEMS LIKE HE'S HAVING A HARD TIME CHANGING BACK.
THIS MUST BE A SIDE EFFECT OF USING ME WITHOUT RESTRICTIONS.
DON'T WORRY, I'M IN A GOOD MOOD RIGHT NOW.
LET'S TALK.

IT'S MOST LIKELY ONLY A MATTER OF TIME, THOUGH...
...SO I'VE BEEN THINKING ABOUT MY NEXT MOVE.
RIP
RIP
?
SHK
PLIP
PLIP
GUSH
WHA-?!
I'M TAKING HIM HOSTAGE!
BADUM
BADUM
BADUM
I CAN LIVE WITH-OUT THIS THING.
PLOP
BUT HE CAN'T!
SWITCHING NOW MEANS HIS DEATH.
ALSO...

JUST TO MAKE SURE.
SUKUNA'S FINGER!!
GULP
IT WAS INSIDE THE SPECIAL GRADE?!
KRAK
NOW THEN...
KRAK
I'M FINALLY FREE.
YOU CAN BE SCARED NOW!
KRAK
THERE'S NO REAL REASON FOR THIS, BUT...
...TIME FOR YOU TO DIE!
THIS IS JUST LIKE LAST TIME...
...EXCEPT NOW THE ROLES ARE REVERSED.

KIYOTAKA IJICHI

(26 YEARS OLD)

• Ijichi is a character who also appears in my earlier series, *Jujutsu High*.

• At that time, he looked like he could fight, but in reality, the assistant manager doesn't know how to fight and is technically forbidden from doing so. He handles simple barriers, supports jujutsu sorcerers with shikigami and gives basic instruction to students who are new to field missions.

• He excels in office work.

• Sending students on dangerous missions, frequently getting into conflicts, being abused by Gojo and other senior members—his heart can't take the stress much longer!

CHAPTER 9:
FEARSOME WOMB,
PART 4

THE ONLY THING FAIR ABOUT LIFE IS HOW UNFAIR IT IS TO EVERY-ONE.

HE DOESN'T HAVE THE GUTS TO END HIS OWN LIFE.
I'M SURE OF IT.
HIS ARM IS HEALED, WHICH MEANS HE CAN USE REVERSE CURSED TECHNIQUE.
SUKUNA IS AN INCARNATION. EVEN IF HE CAN LIVE WITHOUT A HEART, HE HAS TO BE HURT.
FWOOO
I'LL MAKE HIM FIX HIS HEART BEFORE ITADORI CHANGES BACK...
I HAVE TO FORCE HIM INTO THINKING...
...HE NEEDS A BODY WITH A HEART TO WIN.
CAN I DO IT?
BUT I COULDN'T EVEN DO ANYTHING AGAINST A SPECIAL GRADE...

IT'S NOT A MATTER OF CAN...
I WILL!!
VWNNN
ALL RIGHT! SINCE WE'RE OUTSIDE...
...LET'S GO ALL OUT.

TP
FOOSH
INTERESTING. A SHIKIGAMI USER WHO...
...ISN'T AFRAID TO MIX IT UP!
BAP
BAP
BAP

YOU GOTTA FEEL THE CURSE MORE!
PAP
KRAK
VNNN
GREAT SERPENT
CHOMP
A AH

KRKL
KRKL
THWAK
DON'T LET UP!

KRRIP
LIKE I SAID...
LET'S GO ALL OUT!
SHP
SPLAT SPLAT SPLAT

FWOOOSH
IT'S NOT JUST HIS JUJUTSU SORCERY, BUT HIS IMMENSE PHYSICAL STRENGTH TOO!
GAH!
VWOOOO
HIS AGILITY!

AK
FWK
FWK
HE'S ON A DIFFERENT LEVEL!!
ZOOSH
WHAT A GREAT CURSED TECH-NIQUE!

CHCHF
NUE IS AT ITS LIMIT.
I BETTER RETURN IT BEFORE IT BREAKS.
I'VE USED ALL OF MY SHIKIGAMI JUST TRYING TO GET OUT OF THIS SITUATION.
PLUS, DIVINE DOGS AND GREAT SERPENT HAVE BEEN DESTROYED.
MY CURSED ENERGY...
VOOM

YOUR SHIKIGAMI...
...USE SHADOWS AS AN INTER-MEDIARY, RIGHT?
KNOWING THAT DOESN'T CHANGE ANYTHING.
SO WHAT?
HMPH...
RATHER THAN USING COMMON TALISMANS, THIS CURSED TECHNIQUE IS MUCH MORE PRACTICAL.
I DON'T GET IT.
BACK THEN...
BOOM
FWOO
...WHY DID YOU RUN AWAY?
?
THAT WAS A WASTED OPPOR-TUNITY.
ANY-WAY...
AT THIS RATE...
...I AIN'T GONNA FIX HIS HEART.

HE READ ME LIKE A BOOK.
I PUT MY LIFE ON THE LINE FOR NOTHING.
WOBBLE
THIS BRAT'S...
...NOT WORTH THE EFFORT.
THEN WHY...
...DID I SAVE HIM?!
THE ONLY THING THAT IS FAIR ABOUT LIFE IS HOW UNFAIR IT IS TO EVERYONE.
IF I'VE GOT THE TIME TO CURSE SOME-ONE...
...I'D RATHER SPEND IT THINKING OF THOSE I HOLD DEAR.

SHE WAS THE KINDEST PERSON. THERE WAS NO REASON TO THINK OTHERWISE. SHE WAS SOMEONE WHO DESERVED TO BE HAPPY.
BUT TSUMIKI WAS CURSED.
MY FATHER, WHO DIDN'T EVEN KNOW MY GENDER, GAVE ME THE NAME MEGUMI. HE'S STILL ALIVE SOMEWHERE.
KARMA DOESN'T HAPPEN ON ITS OWN.
CRIMINALS ARE DISCIPLINED UNDER THE LAW.
JUJUTSU SORCERERS ARE ONLY A COG IN THIS RETRIBUTION.
IF ONLY MORE GOOD PEOPLE...
...COULD RECEIVE FAIRNESS.

I'LL SAVE PEOPLE...
...WHETHER OR NOT IT'S FAIR!
KZZT
KZZT
KZZT
GOOD.
THAT'S IT.
YOU'RE FINALLY READY TO GO ALL OUT!

SHOW ME WHAT YOU GOT...
...MEGUMI FUSHIGURO!
WITH THIS TREASURE, I SUMMON...
PZZZT...
EIGHT HANDLES—
!
FSHHH
I...

I DIDN'T SAVE YOU...
...BECAUSE IT WAS THE LOGICAL THING TO DO.
I DIDN'T WANT TO SEE A GOOD PERSON, NO MATTER HOW DANGEROUS, DIE.
I DID HAVE TO THINK ABOUT IT.
IN THE END, IT WAS A SELFISH, EMOTIONAL DECISION.
BUT THAT'S OKAY.
I'M NOT A HERO.
I'M A JUJUTSU SORCERER.

THAT'S WHY I'VE NEVER REGRETTED SAVING YOU.
NOT EVEN FOR A MOMENT.
I SEE...
FSH...
YOU'RE SO SMART, FUSHIGURO.
THINKING ABOUT ALL SORTS OF STUFF, UNLIKE ME.
I THINK YOUR WAY OF DOING THINGS IS ALSO RIGHT.
BUT THAT DOESN'T MEAN MINE ISN'T.
...

PLIP
OH! SORRY ...
TIME'S UP.
PLIP
FUSHIGURO, AS FOR YOU, KUGISAKI...
WORMP...
...AND GOJO SENSEI... WELL, GUESS I DON'T HAVE TO WORRY ABOUT HIM.
LIVE A LONG LIFE, OKAY?
THUD

In the language of
flowers, a lily represents
"purity and innocence."
A black lily represents
a "curse"...

Apparently.

WAS IT NECESSARY TO USE A PRECIOUS FINGER...
...JUST TO GET THAT INFORMATION...
CHAPTER 10: AFTER THE RAIN
GLUG GLUG
...ABOUT SUKUNA'S POWER?
WE CAN'T TAKE HALF MEASURES WITH THIS.
WE GOT SOME VALUABLE INFORMATION.
PUFF
PUFF
HMPH!
I HOPE THAT'S NOT AN EXCUSE.

YOU! SHUT UP!
I CAN'T UNDERSTAND WHAT YOU'RE SAYING, BUT I CAN HEAR THE MEANING IN MY HEAD! IT'S CREEPY!
BOOF
GHOSTO
GHOSTO
2F
Cafe Restaurant
GHOSTO
RING
RING
WEL-COME!
PARTY OF ONE?
YES.
ONLY ONE.

IT WAS INTENTIONAL, WASN'T IT?
WHAT DO YOU MEAN?
BADUM
BADUM
THE ENEMY WAS SPECIAL GRADE. FIVE RESCUE TARGETS WHO WEREN'T EVEN CONFIRMED ALIVE.
THERE'S NO WAY I'D SEND IN FIRST-YEARS FOR THAT.

I HAD TO PULL SOME STRINGS TO GET A STAY OF EXECUTION FOR ITADORI.
THOSE CRUSTY HIGHER-UPS USED THE SPECIAL GRADE TO GET RID OF HIM IN MY ABSENCE.
IF THE OTHER TWO HAD DIED, THAT WOULD HAVE BEEN THE ICING ON THE CAKE, RIGHT?
BUT WHEN THE MISSION WAS PLANNED...
SHAKA SHAKA
...THERE WAS NO INDICATION OF A SPECIAL GRADE.
WHAT A PAIN FINDING THE CULPRIT.
MAYBE I SHOULD JUST...
...KILL ALL THE HIGHER-UPS!

YOU'RE BEING EMOTIONAL FOR ONCE!
!
YOU REALLY HAD A SOFT SPOT FOR HIM, HUH?
SURE. I'M A NICE GUY WHO LOOKS OUT FOR HIS STUDENTS.
JUJUTSU HIGH DOCTOR SHOKO IEIRI
DON'T PICK ON IJICHI TOO MUCH.
HE'S CAUGHT IN THE MIDDLE BETWEEN US AND THE HIGHER-UPS.
BLUSH
SAY MORE...
SO...
THIS IS...
SHP
I DON'T CARE ABOUT HIS HARD-SHIPS.
I SEE.
SAY MORE!!

...SUKUNA'S VESSEL.
FWISH
I CAN DISSECT HIM ANY WAY I WANT, RIGHT?
YOU BETTER MAKE IT WORTH IT.
I WILL.
WHO DO YOU THINK I AM?
HE TOLD US TO LIVE A LONG LIFE...

WHAT USE IS HE DEAD?
HEY... IS THIS THE FIRST TIME A FRIEND OF YOURS HAS DIED?
A CLASS-MATE, YEAH...
REALLY? BUT YOU SEEM FINE.
LOOKS WHO'S TALKING.
OF COURSE, I'VE ONLY KNOWN HIM FOR TWO WEEKS.
I'M NOT THE KIND OF GIRL...
...WHO CRIES OVER A GUY LIKE THAT.

FSSSHH
MAN, IT'S HOT!
YEAH... I WONDER WHEN WE'LL GET OUR SUMMER UNIFORMS.
SHEESH... YOU'RE MORE MOODY THAN USUAL...
MEGUMI.
WHAT IS THIS, A FUNERAL?!
ZEN'IN SENPAI...
DON'T YOU DARE CALL ME BY MY LAST—
MAKI.
MAKI!!

HE REALLY DID DIE.
IT HAPPENED YESTERDAY! A FIRST-YEAR BOY!!
FISH FLAKES!!
YOU
DRIP DRIP
ARE A
LIT-TLE LATE!
DRIP DRIP
NOW I LOOK LIKE A COLD-HEARTED DEMON!
WELL, YOU PRETTY MUCH ARE!
RAWWR
TUNA MAYO.

RAHH
RAH
WHO ARE THOSE PEOPLE?
CHATTER CHATTER
OUR SCHOOL'S UPPER-CLASS-MEN.
YAAA YAA
THAT'S ZEN'IN SENPAI.
OUT OF ALL THE STUDENTS HERE, NOBODY'S A BETTER CURSED-TOOL USER THAN HER.
IS TAKING IT EASY ON THEM REALLY KINDNESS?
JUJUTSU HIGH SECOND-YEAR MAKI ZEN'IN
THIS IS INUMAKI SENPAI.
HE'S A CURSED-SPEECH USER.
SALTED SALMON ROE!
THE ONLY WORDS HE SAYS ARE RICE-BALL FILLINGS.
JUJUTSU HIGH SECOND-YEAR TOGE INUMAKI
AND PANDA SENPAI.
BUT WHEN SHE'S WITH YUTA...
...SHE'S KIND OF NICE.
JUJUTSU HIGH SECOND-YEAR PANDA

OKKOTSU SENPAI ISN'T HERE, BUT HE'S THE ONLY ONE WHO I CAN SINCERELY RESPECT.
HE'S ABROAD RIGHT NOW.
YOU GONNA ELABORATE ON PANDA? OR IS HE JUST, YOU KNOW, A PANDA?
SORRY 'BOUT THIS...
...ESPECIALLY DURING THIS SAD TIME.
FORGIVE US.
BUT WE WANT YOU GUYS...
...TO PARTICIPATE IN THE KYOTO SISTER-SCHOOL GOODWILL EVENT.
KYOTO SISTER-SCHOOL GOODWILL EVENT?
IT'S A GOODWILL EVENT WITH THE OTHER JUJUTSU HIGH IN KYOTO.
BUT ISN'T IT USUALLY SECOND- AND THIRD-YEARS WHO PARTICIPATE?
YEAH YEAH

THAT IDIOT THIRD-YEAR IS SUSPENDED RIGHT NOW.
WE DON'T HAVE ENOUGH PEOPLE, SO YOU GUYS ARE IN.
WHAT DO WE DO IN THE EVENT?
SMASH BROS.?
I'M GOOD AT THE WII VERSION. METEOR SMASH ALL THE WAY.
ACTUALLY, MAYBE THE THREE OF US IS FINE.
TOKYO HIGH. KYOTO HIGH.
OVER THE COURSE OF TWO DAYS...
...EACH PRINCIPAL CHOOSES AN EVENT FOR THE DAY.
BUT THAT'S OVER-SIMPLIFYING IT.
EVERY YEAR FOLLOWS THE SAME PATTERN— THE FIRST DAY IS THE TEAM EVENT AND THE SECOND DAY THE INDIVIDUAL EVENT.
SALMON.
INDI-VIDUAL AND TEAM EVENTS...
...AGAINST OTHER JUJUTSU SORCER-ERS?!

YUP!
A JUJUTSU BATTLE WHERE "NO KILLING" IS THE ONLY RULE.
HEH
WE'LL MAKE SURE TO GET YOU GUYS IN TIP-TOP SHAPE SO YOU DON'T DIE.
FWSH
FWSH
HM?
DO WE HAVE THE TIME?
WE'RE LOW ON JUJUTSU SORCERERS, RIGHT?
GOO-OOD...
...QUES-TION!
RIGHT NOW...
PEOPLE'S DEPRESSION DURING THE WINTER AND SPRING SEASONS...
WINTER
AUTONOMIC
CHANGING OF
STRESS
DEC-FEB
MAR
APRIL
...MANIFESTS AS CURSES IN HUGE QUANTITIES DURING THE SUMMER.
IT'S THE BUSY SEASON, SO TO SPEAK.
WE'RE QUADRUPLETS!

THERE ARE TIMES WHEN IT'S BUSY ALL YEAR.
IT'S PROBABLY GONNA CALM DOWN A LITTLE THOUGH.
HM...
SO?
YOU'RE IN, RIGHT?
DO IT FOR YOUR FALLEN FRIEND!
WE'RE IN!

I WILL ...
I WILL ...
...BECOME STRONGER.
I'LL DO ANYTHING IT TAKES.
BUT IF I THINK...
...BOTH THE TRAINING AND EVENT ARE POINTLESS, I'M OUT.
SAME.
HEH...
IT SHOULD BE FUN PUTTING YOU GUYS IN YOUR PLACE.
FISH FLAKES.

RINK BAR
SO, YOUR BOSS...
...WANTS TO REVERSE THE ROLES OF CURSES AND HUMANS IN THIS WORLD.
IS THAT RIGHT?
NOT.
QUITE.
Tp
HUMANS ARE MADE OF LIES.
THERE'S ALWAYS A FLIP SIDE TO THE POSITIVE EMOTIONS THEY SHOW.
BUT NEGATIVE EMO-TIONS...
...SUCH AS HATRED AND KILLING INTENT... THOSE ARE PURE TRUTHS.
CURSES BORN FROM SUCH TRUTHS ARE...

BUBBLE
BUBBLE
...THE PUREST FORM!
WE'RE THE TRUE HUMANS!
THE FAKE ONES...
...SHOULD BE BURNED AWAY!
BUT THE REALITY IS...
...YOU'LL BE THE ONES WHO DISAPPEAR.
THAT'S WHY WE'RE ASKING...
...FOR HELP DEFEATING THE JUJUTSU SORCERERS.
BEFORE THE WAR...
...YOU'LL NEED TO MEET TWO CONDITIONS TO WIN.

FIRST, IMMOBILIZE SATORU GOJO AND REMOVE HIM FROM THE FIGHT.
AND SECOND, MAKE AN ALLY OF RYOMEN SUKUNA AND YUJI ITADORI.
ISN'T YUJI ITADORI ...
...DEAD?
DON'T BE SO SURE...
...ABOUT THAT.

DON'T LOOK UP AT ME WITHOUT PERMISSION.
IT'S ANNOYING.
YOU BRAT!
THEN GET DOWN HERE...
KRK
...SO I CAN LOOK DOWN ON YA!

SHOKO IEIRI

(28 YEARS OLD)

- Shoko was in the same year and class as Gojo.
- She's one of a few people who can heal by using reverse cursed technique, so she's incredibly valuable.
- After high school, she obtained her doctor's license in two years by cheating.
- She doesn't like sweets, but she loves alcohol.
- She quit smoking five years ago.

YOU KNOW...
...I HAVE A LOUSY PERSON-ALITY.
CHAPTER 11: A DREAM
I KNOW.
ZING
IJICHI, YOU'RE IN FOR A SERIOUS FACE SLAP LATER.
SERIOUS FACE SLAP?
I'M JUST NOT THE TEACHER TYPE, SO WHY WOULD SOMEONE LIKE ME BE AT A PLACE LIKE JUJUTSU HIGH?
WHY?
I HAVE A DREAM.

YOU LOOK LIKE YOU WANT TO KILL ME.
I WONDER WHY. YOU DID JUST KILL ME.
AREN'T YOU FORGETTING TO THANK ME FOR FIXING YOUR ARM?
SIGH...
BUT YOU RIPPED OUT MY HEART AFTER THAT!
DO I HAVE TO SPEND THE AFTERLIFE WITH YOU TOO?
IS THIS HELL?
SHP
IF THAT'S THE CASE, THEN...
I'LL MAKE YOU CRY!
FSH

VOOM
KRAK
VWOOO
TMP

!
TMP TMP TMP TMP
BETTER GRIT YOUR TEETH!
UNNECES-SARY.
FWP

WHIFF
GOING FOR MY FOOTING, HUH?
TMBL
PSYCH!
GOTCHA!

FWISH
HUH?
HOW BORING.
WHAK
ACK!
SPLAASH

BAH!
SPLISH
I THOUGHT I HAD HIM.
KERSP
LASH
GUH!
PLOOP
THIS IS MY *INNATE DOMAIN.*
THIS WORLD ISN'T WHAT YOU THINK IT IS.
TUNK
GLUG GLUG GLUG

?
FUSHIGURO MENTIONED THAT, I THINK...
THINK OF IT AS BEING "INSIDE" THE HEART.
IDIOT.
IN OTHER WORDS ...
WE'RE...
...NOT DEAD... YET!
IF YOU ACCEPT MY TERMS...
...I'LL FIX YOUR HEART AND REVIVE YOU.
LOOK AT YOU.
TALKING ALL BIG, BUT YOU WANNA LIVE TOO, HUH?
THE GAME HAS CHANGED.
SOON...
...WE'LL SEE SOMETHING INTERESTING.

I HAVE TWO CONDI-TIONS.
① YOU AGREE TO LET ME TAKE OVER YOUR BODY FOR ONE FULL MINUTE WHEN I CHANT "ENCHAIN."
AND ② YOU WILL FORGET ABOUT THIS AGREEMENT.
NO WAY.
I'M NOT SURE WHAT YOU'RE AFTER, BUT THAT'S TOO FISHY.
I KNOW FOR SURE NOW.
YOU'RE EVIL. I WON'T EVER LET YOU USE MY BODY AGAIN.
WHAT IF I PROMISE I WON'T KILL OR HURT ANYONE DURING THAT MINUTE?
WILL THAT DO?
SHEESH...
LIKE I'D BELIEVE YOU!
IT DOESN'T MATTER IF YOU BELIEVE ME OR NOT.
THIS IS A BINDING VOW.
I'M THE ONE WHO WILL BE PUNISHED IF I BREAK IT.

THERE ARE CONSEQUENCES FOR BEING GREEDY.
IT WAS FINE BEFORE!
I WANTED TO CHANGE BACK THEN TOO.
YOU DID AS YOU WERE TOLD BY THAT JUJUTSU SORCERER.
THAT JUJUTSU SORCERER
YOU KNOW THAT BETTER THAN ANYONE ELSE.
A BINDING VOW IS BASED ON MUTUAL INTERESTS.
IT'S IMPORTANT IN THE WORLD OF JUJUTSU.
I DON'T KNOW WHAT YOU'RE AFTER...
...BUT IT MEANS I CAN BE REVIVED, RIGHT?
FINE. I ACCEPT.
NOW GET OFFA ME!

WHAK
LIKE I'D SAY THAT!
REVIVE ME WITHOUT ANY CONDITIONS.
YOU'RE THE ONE WHO GOT ME KILLED, AFTER ALL.
SPLASH
SPLASH

THEN HOW ABOUT THIS...
A FIGHT TO THE DEATH.
IF YOU WIN, NO CONDITIONS. IF I WIN, I REVIVE YOU WITH THE BINDING VOW.
OKAY!
I'M GONNA KICK YOUR—
FWIK
A DREAM?
YUP.
AS THEY MADE CLEAR WITH YUJI, THE HIGHER-UPS ARE THE SCUM OF THE JUJUTSU WORLD.
SELFISH IDIOTS, BLOODLINE IDIOTS, PROUD IDIOTS—JUST PLAIN IDIOTS!

I'M GONNA RESET...
...THIS CRAPPY JUJUTSU WORLD!
IT'D BE EASY TO KILL EVERYONE WHO'S IN CHARGE.
BUT SOMEONE ELSE WOULD JUST TAKE THEIR PLACE. NOTHING WOULD CHANGE.
AND IT'S NOT AS IF PEOPLE APPROVE OF MASSACRES ANYWAY...
...SO THAT'S WHY I'M TURNING TO EDUCATION.
I NEED STRONG AND INTELLIGENT ALLIES.
I NEED TO FOSTER THEM!

TO THAT END, I'LL SOMETIMES ASSIGN MY MISSIONS TO THEM.
TOUGH LOVE.
YOU SURE YOU AREN'T JUST LAZY?
THEY'RE ALL GREAT.
ESPECIALLY THIRD-YEAR HAKARI AND SECOND-YEAR OKKOTSU.
THEY'LL BE AS GOOD AS ME SOMEDAY.
SKWEEZ
YUJI WAS NO EXCEPTION.
HEY, YOU GUYS.
I'M ABOUT TO GET STARTED.
YOU JUST GONNA SIT THERE AND WATCH?

WHOA!
FULL FRONTAL!
G-G-G-GOJO!
H-H-HE'S ALIVE!
HEH HEH ...
SHUT UP, IJICHI.
UM, THIS IS KINDA EMBARRASSING.
WHO ARE YOU?
TOO BAD.
YUJI!
WEL-COME BACK!

YO!
I'M BACK!
WH
AP!
OH, RIGHT. I HAVE TO CHANGE THE REPORT.
NO, LEAVE IT AS IS.
BEFORE HE'S TARGETED AGAIN, I'D LIKE TO AT LEAST GIVE YUJI SOME BASIC TRAINING.
PLEASE LEAVE HIM LISTED AS DECEASED IN THE REPORT.
HM?

THEN ITADORI WILL HAVE TO GO INTO HIDING FOR GOOD.
NAH, I'LL HAVE HIM READY IN TIME FOR THE GOODWILL EVENT.
WHY?
EASY.
I REFUSE TO KEEP THIS KID...
I WONDER IF EVERY-ONE WILL BE SUR-PRISED.
...FROM LIVING THE BEST YEARS OF HIS LIFE.
NOT JUST HIM, BUT EVERYONE.

KLINK
SATORU GOJO.
SO EVEN IF WE WORK TOGETHER, WE WOULDN'T BE ABLE TO KILL HIM?
YOU MIGHT BE ABLE TO RUN AWAY. WORST CASE, HE'D EXORCISE YOU ALL.
INSTEAD OF TRYING TO *KILL* HIM, FOCUS ON *SEALING* HIM.
SEALING?
HOW?
USE A SPECIAL GRADE CURSED ITEM...
...LIKE PRISON REALM.

The wide-sleeve design of Sukuna's kimono is usually for women. It's probably easier for him to move his four arms around in than in his previous life.

I WILL BE FLAKING OUT ON MY JOB.
CHAPTER 12: PUSHING FORWARD
I'VE ALWAYS BEEN THE RESPONSIBLE TYPE.
MOST OF MY PAY GOES TOWARD SAVING UP TO HELP SEND MY FOUR YOUNGER SISTERS-IN-LAW TO COLLEGE.
EVEN A MAN LIKE ME...
...CAN'T DENY THIS PRIMAL SENSE OF FEAR.
IF I GET CLOSE TO THAT TABLE...
...I'LL DIE!!

PRISON REALM ...?
BLUB BLUB BLUB
YOU HAVE IT?!
PUFF PUFF
THAT TABOO OBJECT ?!
CALM DOWN, JOGO.
IT'S GETTING HOT.
TABLE FIVE ISN'T ORDERING AT ALL.
HE'S HOGGING A TABLE TO HIMSELF.
SOMEONE GO AND HURRY HIM UP.
HUH?
WHAT ?!
HEY!
WAIT A SECOND!
FOOSH
SORRY BOSS ...
...I QUIT.

WANT ME TO GO?
IT'S FINE.
FAN FAN
IS THE A.C. WORKING?
...?
SIR, ARE YOU READY TO OR...
...DER?
BOOF
AHHHHHHHHHHHHHH!
I'D RATHER YOU NOT CAUSE A COM-MOTION.
HOW ABOUT THIS?
FWP

BOOF
BOBOOF
BOOF
SZZ
ZZ
GOOD THING I DIDN'T CHOOSE AN EXPENSIVE RESTAURANT.
KOFF
GETO.
HOW STRONG AM I IN TERMS OF SUKUNA FINGERS?

BEING GENEROUS ...
...I'D SAY ABOUT EIGHT OR NINE.
GIVE ME PRISON REALM! I'LL ADD IT TO THE COLLECTION!
IN EX-CHANGE ...
THAT'S PLENTY!
...I'LL KILL...
... SATORU GOJO!
C-3
B-3
BY THE TIME WE GOT TO THE SCENE...
...YOUR SON WAS ALREADY DEAD.

TO BE HONEST, I WASN'T SURE ABOUT...
...SAVING PEOPLE IN THAT FACILITY.
BUT MY FRIENDS THOUGHT OTHERWISE.
WE WEREN'T ABLE TO SAVE HIM. EVEN AFTER WE CONFIRMED HIS DEATH...
...THEY TRIED TO BRING BACK HIS BODY.

RRRIP
UNFOR-TUNATELY, THE BODY...
...DISINTE-GRATED ALONG WITH THE SPECIAL GRADE'S INNATE DOMAIN.
I MANAGED TO...
...GET THIS.
TADASHI OKAZAKI
I'M SORRY WE COULDN'T...
...SAVE TADASHI'S LIFE.

PLEASE, DON'T APOLOGIZE.
I'M THE ONLY PERSON...
...WHO WILL GRIEVE FOR HIM.
DUN DUN DUN DUN
YOU'RE LATE, MEGUMI!
KELP.
WHERE WERE YOU?
DOES IT MATTER?
STARE

ZEN'IN SENPAI...
AS A JUJUTSU SORCERER, WHAT KIND OF PEOPLE DO YOU WANT TO SAVE?
HUH?
I DON'T THINK ABOUT IT.
I WASTED MY TIME ASKING.
MUMBLE
WHAT ?!
FUSHI-GURO!
WHAT'RE YOU DOING, CONDUCTING AN INTERVIEW OVER THERE?!
GRMBL GRMBL
TRADE PLACES WITH ME! THIS SCHOOL UNIFORM IS A PAIN. I'M GONNA GO BUY A CUTE TRACKSUIT!
GRMBL GRMBL
AHHHHH
GYAA
WHAT ARE THOSE TWO DOING?
TOSS
YOU GUYS ARE WEAK IN CLOSE COMBAT.
FIRST, TRY AND WIN AGAINST ME.
FWISH

THEN WE'LL TALK.
TP
YUJI, YOU'RE BETTER THAN MOST WHEN IT COMES TO CLOSE COMBAT...
...BUT RIGHT NOW, YOU'VE GOT TO LEARN...
...HOW TO CONTROL CURSED ENERGY.
AND YOU NEED TO LEARN A BIT OF JUJUTSU.
WHAT'S UP?
WOO HOO
IT'S JUST THAT IF I'M GONNA LEARN...
...I'M GLAD IT'S FROM YOU, GOJO SENSEI.
HEH HEH

I'M WEAK AND COULDN'T HELP ANYONE.
I EVEN ALMOST GOT FUSHIGURO KILLED.
I CAN'T SEE THEM YET, NOT THE WAY I AM NOW.
I WANT TO BECOME STRONG.
PLEASE TEACH ME HOW TO BECOME THE *STRONGEST!*
DON'T WORRY.
I'M THE STRONGEST.
PLEASE PAY ATTENTION TO THE CANS OVER THERE, THANK YOU.
HEH HEH...
YOU'VE GOT A GOOD EYE.
YOU'RE THE ONE WHO DUBBED YOURSELF THE STRONGEST!

FWAK
KRUNCH
KRUNCH
KRUNCH
WHOA!
KLANK
THIS IS CURSED ENERGY.
AND THIS IS CURSED TECHNIQUE.
DRIP
RIGHT, I DON'T GET IT.
OKAY, LET'S SEE...
THINK OF CURSED ENERGY AS ELECTRICITY...
...AND CURSED TECHNIQUE AS ELECTRONICS.

IT'S DIFFICULT TO USE ELECTRICITY BY ITSELF, RIGHT?
SO YOU USE ELECTRICITY TO *POWER* ELECTRONICS. THIS WAY YOU CAN GAIN A VARIETY OF USES.
I JUST HIT THIS WITH CURSED ENERGY.
AS FOR THIS, CURSED ENERGY FLOWED IN A TECHNIQUE...
...TO ACTIVATE IT. THEN I USED JUJUTSU TO TWIST THE CAN.
THAT MEANS...
...I'M GONNA LEARN A BADASS CURSED TECHNIQUE!
DING
NOPE.
YOU'RE UNABLE TO USE JUJUTSU, YUJI.

OTHER THAN SIMPLE SHIKIGAMI OR BARRIERS...
...THE ABILITY TO USE CURSED TECHNIQUES IS INTRINSIC.
SO A JUJUTSU SORCERER'S SKILL SET IS ABOUT 80 PERCENT INNATE TALENT.
NO INNATE TALENT
YOU OKAY?
I JUST THOUGHT I COULD USE THUNDER, OR FIRE, OR MAYBE A POWER BOMB.
DISAPPOINTED
YOU CAN STILL DO A POWER BOMB.
YOU A WRESTLER?
YOU'RE UNABLE TO USE IT NOW.
FORGET ABOUT THAT. FOR NOW, LET'S FOCUS ON IMPROVING YOUR STRENGTHS.
WE'LL APPLY CURSED ENERGY TO YOUR PHYSICAL ATTACKS!
UGH...
IN DUE TIME, YOUR BODY...
AH... I'M DONE FOR.
...WILL LEARN SUKUNA'S CURSED TECHNIQUE!

RATHER THAN SOME HALF-ASSED CURSED TECHNIQUE...
JOLT
...I'M MORE WARY OF SAVAGE ATTACKS.
LIKE I SAID BEFORE ...
...YOU'RE AWESOME IN PHYSICAL FIGHTS.
I'M BACK!
HOLD ON!
FSH
I ALREADY KNOW HOW TO DO THAT!
GET UP.
THAT TIME, I KIND OF...
...GOT IT.
THEN DO IT AGAIN.
HERE.
PUNCH RIGHT HERE.
IT'S NOT LIKE YOU CAN ANYWAY.

DON'T BLAME ME IF YOU GET HURT!
FSH
YEAH, YEAH.
HURRY UP.
FWISH
POP

I DIDN'T FEEL ANY...
...CURSED ENERGY.
WHY?!
THE BASIS OF CURSED ENERGY IS NEGATIVE EMOTION.
WHEN YOU MENTIONED THAT OTHER TIME, YOU WERE OVERWHELMED WITH ANGER AND FEAR, RIGHT?
DING
OH!!
WHEN USING CURSED ENERGY, I'VE ALWAYS GOTTA BE MAD!
FUSHIGURO ALWAYS SEEMS A LITTLE TICKED OFF TOO!
TUMP
NOPE.
JOLT

WHAT'S WRONG?
SOMETHING REALLY ANNOYED ME JUST NOW.
YOU LITTLE...!
AAGHHHHH
NO, NOT YOU.
THERE'S A MONTH AND A HALF UNTIL THE EVENT.
DON'T GET DISTRACTED.
HERE, TRY THE POLE ARM NEXT.
PSH
HM... THIS ACTUALLY FEELS RIGHT.
EVERY JUJUTSU SORCERER IS TRAINED TO CONTROL THEIR EMOTIONS WHEN CHANNELING CURSED ENERGY.

SO WHEN THEY'RE OVERWHELMED WITH EMOTION...
...THEY TRY NOT TO WASTE CURSED ENERGY.
THERE ARE MANY WAYS TO TRAIN FOR THIS.
I'M GONNA HAVE YOU DO A PARTICULARLY TOUGH ONE.
GULP
LIKE WHAT?
WATCHING MOVIES!
WATCHING-ING...
...MOVIES?!

WHAT IS...

REVERSE CURSED TECHNIQUE?

• I plan on explaining this eventually in the manga, but I thought I'd give a sneak peek to those of you who bought this volume! (It's not something to get excited over though.)

• As you know, cursed energy comes from negative emotions. Negative emotions are basically stressful, so it's not fit for healing living things. (There are stories of people who get holes in their stomach from too much stress.)

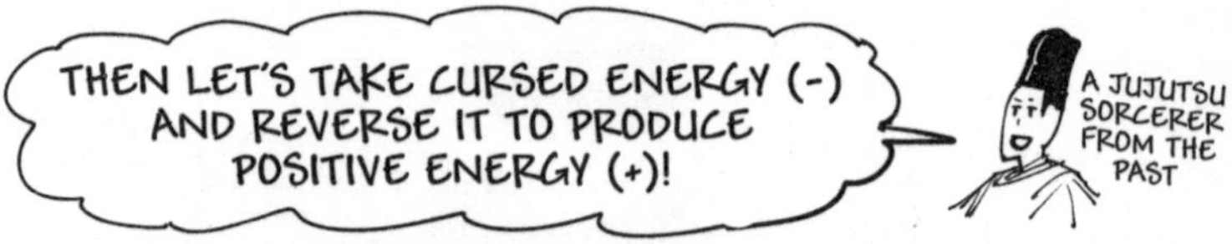

• So now we take what we learned in junior high math:

Negative x Negative = Positive

⇩

Cursed Energy (-) x Cursed Energy (-) = Positive Energy (+)

This cursed energy multiplication is Reverse cursed technique!

⟶ Continued in part 2

WATCHING MOVIES?!
CHAPTER 13: WATCHING MOVIES
YUP.
FROM THE CLASSICS TO NICHE HORROR FILMS TO TRICKY FRENCH FILMS.
EVERY WAKING MOMENT, YOU'RE GONNA WATCH MOVIES.
??
OF COURSE, YOU WON'T BE WATCHING ALONE.
YOU'LL WATCH WITH THIS GUY.
BA
ZZZ

CHAPTER 13: WATCHING MOVIES

WHAT'S WITH THIS UGLY-CUTE DOLL?
CUTE?
(GOJO)
IT'S ONE OF THE PRINCIPAL'S CURSED CORPSES.
I KNEW IT!!
IT'S THE SAME STYLE!
AND?
I'M NOT GETTING ANYTHING FROM IT.
DON'T WORRY. HERE IT COMES.
SWP
WHAK

THAT CURSED CORPSE WILL WAKE UP IF IT DOESN'T RECEIVE A CONSISTENT FLOW OF CURSED ENERGY.
OWWWW
AND IT'LL ATTACK YOU TOO!
LIKE I SAID BEFORE, THERE'S A VARIETY OF MOVIES HERE.
COMEDY. SUSPENSE. ACTION.
THESE MOVIES WILL MAKE YOU CRY, LAUGH AND FEEL SAD.
LET'S START BY WATCHING ONE MOVIE WITHOUT WAKING IT UP.
IN OTHER WORDS, DON'T GET HIT!
PUFF
THIS TRAINING WILL TEACH YOU HOW TO CONTROL THE FLOW OF YOUR CURSED ENERGY UNDER ANY CONDITION.
YOU DON'T WANT TO GIVE IT TOO MUCH OR TOO LITTLE.

VNNN VNNN
SWING SWING
PHEW
ZZZ
JOLT
POP
FOR NOW, IT'S SET TO MATCH YOUR CURSED ENERGY LEVEL, WHICH IS KINDA LOW.
BUT STAY FROSTY. IT'LL SLOWLY REQUIRE A HIGHER FLOW OF CURSED ENERGY OVER TIME.
THERE'S NO WAY I'M GONNA LET UP.
PHEW
SO... WHICH ONE FIRST?
THIS ONE'S MY RECOMMENDATION. THE HEROINE IS SUPER ANNOYING...
...BUT MEETS A GRUESOME DEATH.
POP
SPOILERS, DUDE!

LET'S START WITH AN ACTIO–
NGH!
KRUNCH
AGGGHH! DAMMIT!!
BOINK
HEY, EVEN IF YOU'RE FRUSTRATED, KEEP YOUR CURSED ENERGY STEADY!
CARRYING CURSED TOOLS, HUH?
IT'S TRUE THAT THERE ARE ADVANTAGES TO USING THEM IN CLOSE COMBAT.
EVEN A SWORD'S SHEATH IS CUMBERSOME.
BUT I LIKE HAVING MY HANDS FREE CONSIDERING MY CURSED TECHNIQUE.
IT SEEMS LIKE YOU CARRY AT LEAST TWO, ZEN'IN SENPAI.
WHERE DO YOU KEEP THEM?
JUST ASKING.

I MAKE PANDA HOLD ONE.
FLEX
AGAIN... I SHOULDN'T HAVE ASKED.
THERE ARE JUJUTSU SORCERERS WHO USE CURSED SPIRITS TO STORE ITEMS AS WELL.
I'D LOVE THAT.
THEY'RE REALLY RARE, AND YOU ALMOST NEVER SEE THEM USED...
...SINCE IT TAKES A LOT TO TAME THEM.
LET ME KNOW IF YOU FIND ONE.
SURE, FOR A YEAR'S WORTH OF SAUSAGE.
BACK THEN...
...WHY DID YOU RUN?
DID HE MEAN THAT I HAD A CHANCE OF WINNING...
...AGAINST A SPECIAL GRADE?

VNN...
GLOOP
TUNA TUNA.
HUH? WHAT?
SENPAI.
I THINK WE'RE GOOD.

THE RED WIRE OR THE BLUE WIRE... WHICH DO I CUT?!
WHERE I USED TO LIVE, THE GARBAGE BAG COLORS...
WHAT'RE YOU TALKING ABOUT?
BADUM
PLASTICS WERE RED AND COM-BUSTIBLES BLUE...
SIP
BADUM
I WAS THINKING IT WAS THE OTHER WAY AROUND.
BADUM
RED! IT SHOULD BE RED!!
BADUM
BADUM

BIFFF
NOT WHEN I'M DRINKING!
THEN DON'T DRINK!
STOP TAKING IT EASY.
KOFF
KOFF
WATCHING MOVIES IS ALL ABOUT SNACKS AND SODA!
TRUE.
AROUND THAT TIME, KUGISAKI HAD BOUGHT A TRACKSUIT AND WAS GETTING DISTRACTED AROUND TOWN.
I DON'T SEE URAHARA!
WHERE IS IT?
IS IT UNDERGROUND?!

WELL.
I'VE GOTTA RUN.
KEEP IT UP.
WORMP
AM I REALLY GONNA GET STRONGER?
YEAH!
OH, BY THE WAY, DID YOU TALK WITH SUKUNA WHILE YOU WERE DEAD?
TALK...
ANY CONDITIONS OR CONTRACTS IN EXCHANGE FOR FIXING YOUR HEART?
UM... WE TALKED ABOUT SOME-THING.

I DON'T REALLY REMEMBER.
...
I SEE.
VRMM...

THERE'S STILL SOME TIME UNTIL WE HAVE TO MEET THE PRINCIPAL.
NEED A PIT STOP?
NAH, LET'S BE EARLY FOR ONCE.
STOP THE CAR.
UH... HERE?
YOU GO AHEAD.
WHAT?!
AM I BEING TESTED?
LIKE, YOU'LL BEAT ME UP IF I REALLY GO AHEAD.
WHAT DO YOU TAKE ME FOR?
VRMMM...

WELL THEN.

AND YOU...
...ARE?
SHF

TAKE THIS!
FWISH
BL
OP

BOFFFF
GWOOM...
WAS THAT IT?
NOTHING SPECIAL.
SZZZZ
GLOOP GLOOP

WHO'RE YOU CALLING ...
FSHHH
...NOTHING SPECIAL?
HALT
STUPID BRAT.
SQUEAK
I CAN COM-MUNICATE WITH HIM NORMALLY EVEN THOUGH HE'S A CURSED SPIRIT.
ON TOP OF THAT, HIS CURSED ENERGY... IT'S AN UNREG-ISTERED SPECIAL GRADE.

SPECIAL GRADES ARE JUST THAT—SPECIAL.
HE'S PROBABLY STRONGER THAN THE CURRENT SUKUNA.
CAN'T HAVE GUYS LIKE THAT POPPING UP EVERYWHERE.
WHAT'S THE MATTER? LOSING HEART?
NAH...
IT'S STARTING TO GET FUN!
KRAK

WHAT IS...

REVERSE CURSED TECHNIQUE?

PART 2

• Like I said before, healing humans is a difficult technique. However, cursed spirits are made up of cursed energy, so they don't need to use Reverse cursed technique.

← This is what he means.

• While some people are able to use Reverse cursed technique, there others like Sukuna who can reconstruct limbs or heal mild damage for others or themselves.

• "But I thought cursed technique is decided when you're born! You liar, Akutami! Die!!" Some of you might be thinking that, but please calm down. Reverse cursed technique involves the processing of cursed energy. (I'm sorry this is so confusing.)

• The positive (+) energy that comes from Reverse cursed technique for healing uses cursed energy. If you use this instead of negative (-) cursed energy to power your inherent cursed technique, you can reverse the effects of your cursed technique. This is what Gojo is referring to when he says "cursed technique reversal" in chapter 14. (So confusing!)

End

THIS IS FUN, HUH?
CHAPTER 14: ASSAULT
YOU HAVE NO SENSE OF DANGER AT ALL.
POP
HE LURED ME OUT TO WHERE THERE'S NO ONE AROUND.
NO, IT'S TO MAKE SURE I CAN'T CALL FOR SUPPORT.
POP POP POP POP

EMBER INSECTS
BUZZ BUZZ
WELL, IT WAS THE RIGHT MOVE TO TARGET ME.
NO SENSE OF DANGER, HUH?
VOOSH

HA
LT
HALT
HALT
HALT
WHAT HAPPENS IF IT STINGS ME?
TP
SKREE
AAAAHHHHH
AAAAAHHHHH

FWP
SHUDDER
SOUND?
SHUDDER
BOOOM

VSSHHH...
COMBINING SONIC AND EXPLOSIVE ATTACKS...?
FSH
NOT BAD.
FWAP

SZZ SZZ
THERE'S MORE!
THUP
BOOOF

IS THAT IT?
SO THAT GUY WAS EXAG-GERATING.
HUMANS THESE DAYS ARE WEAK. THEY DON'T LIVE IN TRUTH.
FSHHH
Deplorable.
Makes me sick.
REAL STRENGTH.
AND THE TRUTH.
FWAP
THROUGH DEATH, IT WILL BE SPREAD.
THIS AGAIN?

WHEN ARE YOU GONNA LEARN?
FSH
SO SMOKY.
HOW–?
UM...THE SHORT VERSION?
IT DIDN'T HIT ME.
YOU'RE LYING! THAT'S NOT WHAT I SAW.
I KILLED YOU!
KSSH
WHAT YOU TOUCHED...
...WAS THE *INFINITY* BETWEEN US.

?
HERE, I'LL SHOW YA. PUT OUT YOUR HAND.
BAM
!
...
THERE'S NO KILLING INTENT... IT CAN'T HURT TO FIND OUT.
HALT
SEE?
I CAN'T TOUCH HIM! MY HAND STOPS JUST BEFORE...
THIS IS INFINITY?

I'M NOT STOPPING YOU. IT'S MORE LIKE YOU'RE SLOWING DOWN THE CLOSER YOU GET.
SO, WHADDAYA THINK?
WANNA...
...HOLD HANDS?
TP...
NO, THANKS.
KRIK
DON'T BE SHY.

YOU'RE MAKING ME FEEL EMBAR-RASSED.
FSH
WHY YOU-!
THH
WAK

SO FAST!!
IT'S NOT JUST A CURSED ENERGY-INFUSED ATTACK!
WHAT IS IT?!
I DON'T UNDERSTAND IT, BUT I HAVE TO!
THERE'S MORE.
HALT
THWA
THWAK
THWAK

INFINITY IS SOMETHING THAT'S NATURALLY THERE.
I JUST BRING IT INTO REALITY.
CURSED
CONVERGENCE AND DIVERGENCE...
IF YOU TOUCH THIS EMPTY SPACE, WHAT WOULD HAPPEN?
TECHNIQUE REVERSAL
RED

FSHFSHFSH

FWAK
LOOK
LOOK
WHAK

VOOM
RAAHH!

KRAK
OH.
SPLASH
THIS IS THE PERFECT OPPOR-TUNITY.
FSSHHH

SURE, YOU CAN TRY, JOGO, BUT YOU'LL DIE.
HE WASN'T KIDDING.
SPLISH
HEH HEH ...
IF I CAN'T HIT HIM...
...I'LL JUST BRING HIM INTO MY DOMAIN.
...?
WHERE'D HE GO?
SORRY 'BOUT THAT.
FWAH

THANKS FOR WAITING.
WHA—?! WHERE ARE WE?!
!
HE'S ...?!
SUKUNA'S VESSEL!!
YUJI'S GONNA BE SITTING IN ON TODAY'S CLASS.
MT. FUJI!
HIS HEAD IS MT. FUJI!

I'D RATHER NOT WRITE ABOUT THIS!

EXPLANATION

LIMITLESS CURSED TECHNIQUE

• Here I'll explain Satoru Gojo's Limitless cursed technique. (I'll be explaining this one in the manga as well.)

• The reason why I don't want to explain this is because I'm an extreme liberal arts thinker.

• In high school, I failed a basic math test.
The worst part is that until I got my test back, I thought for sure I'd gotten at least 90 percent!
What an idiot...

• Everyone, I'd like to start by asking you to read "Achilles and the Tortoise" and "Infinite Number Series." Or maybe ask a math teacher.

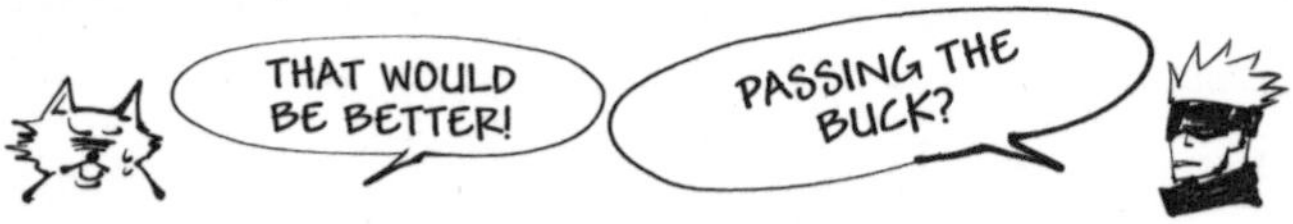

• Gojo's cursed technique is like the convergent infinite number that appears in "Achilles and the Tortoise" brought into reality. However, the infinite number involved with Gojo's cursed technique is fantasy. The repeating addition of numbers gives birth to a fictitious zero and an "unknown" derived from dividing zero. That's why it's called "Limitless."

• Thanks to this, not only can he slow down moving objects, he can create spaces that seem to suck in objects. Create?

→ Continued in part 2

CHAPTER 15: DOMAIN

SAM! SAAAM!
WHERE ARE YOU, SAAAM?!
ZZZ
HM... HE'S ACTUALLY ...
...A PRETTY QUICK LEARNER.
YUJI.
WAH
GOJO SENSEI ?!
THERE'S NO PROBLEM EVEN IF I TALK TO HIM!
WHAT'S UP?!

WE SHOULD UP THE CURSED ENERGY AND MOVE ON TO THE NEXT STEP.
?
LET'S GET OUTTA HERE, YUJI.
HUH ?!
LET'S GO ON A FIELD TRIP TO...
...A HIGH-END JUJUTSU BATTLE.
I'LL TEACH YOU ABOUT...
...DOMAIN EXPANSION.

YUJI'S GONNA BE SITTING IN ON TODAY'S CLASS.
CHAPTER 15: DOMAIN
WASN'T I AT THE SCHOOL JUST, LIKE, TEN SECONDS AGO?
WHAT'S GOING ON?
UM, WE JUMPED.
HE DOESN'T PLAN ON TELLING ME.
SO SUKUNA'S VESSEL IS ALIVE AFTER ALL.
...

FIRST, IMMOBILIZE SATORU GOJO AND REMOVE HIM FROM THE FIGHT.
AND SECOND, MAKE AN ALLY OF RYOMEN SUKUNA AND YUJI ITADORI.
WE NEED ITADORI ALIVE.
DID HE BRING HIM HERE KNOWING OUR PLAN?
WHAT'S WITH THE KID?
GONNA USE HIM AS A SHIELD?
A SHIELD?
NO, NO, NO.
LIKE I SAID, JUST A LITTLE LESSON.
HE'S GOING TO BE A LIABILITY FOR YOU.
YOU FOOL.
I'M IN THE PROCESS OF TEACHING THIS KID A LOT OF THINGS.
SO DON'T WORRY. YOU DO YOUR THING.
WHY AREN'T WE SINKING?

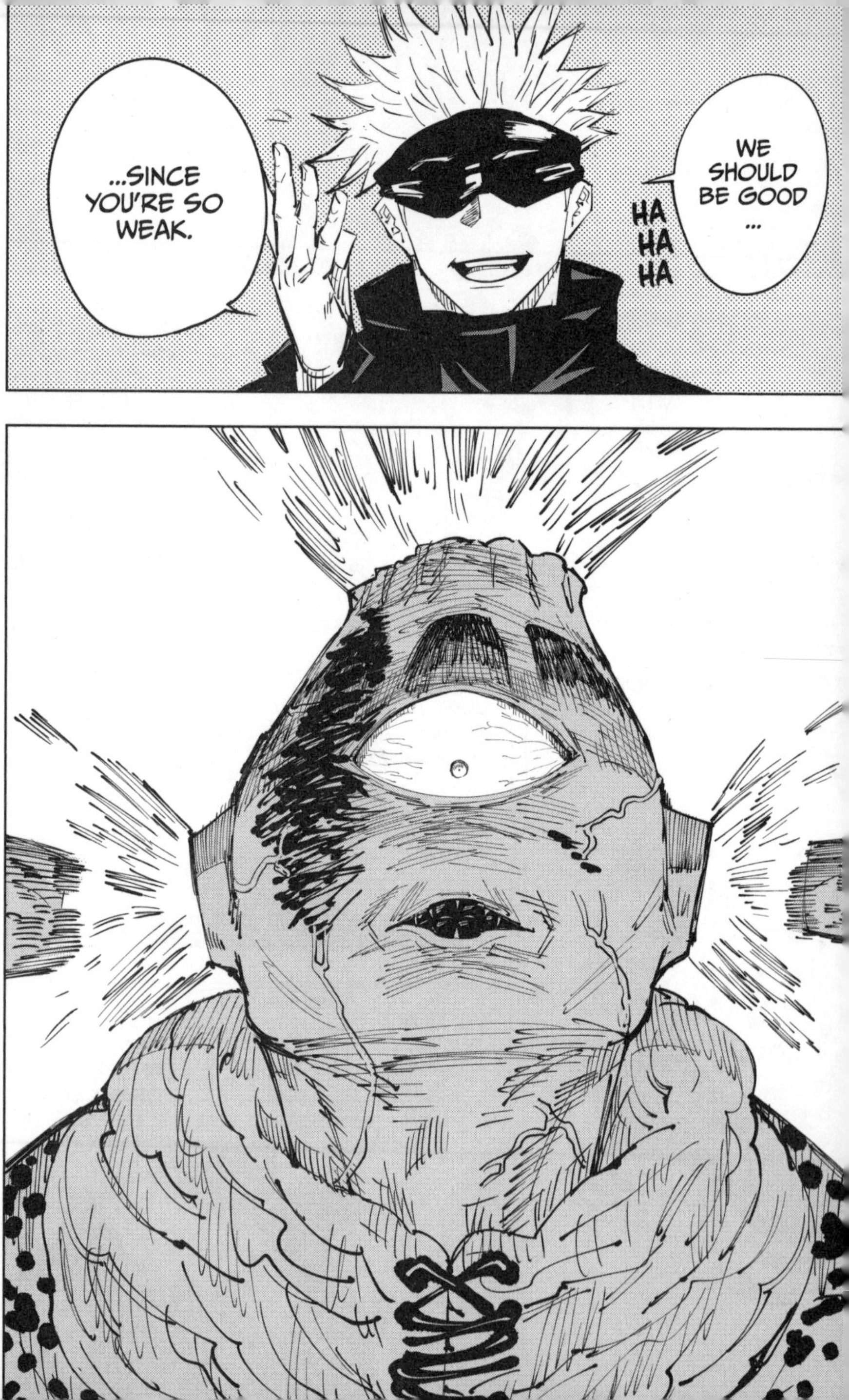
WE SHOULD BE GOOD ...
HA HA HA
...SINCE YOU'RE SO WEAK.

DON'T UNDER-ESTIMATE ME, YOU BRAT!!
BOOF
ROOF
I'LL WRECK YOU AND YOUR SMUG FACE!
SHIVR
SHIVR
SHIVR
SHIVR
HE'S...
...WEAK?
IT'S A MONSTER...
...STRONGER THAN ANY-THING...
...I'VE SEEN BEFORE!!
PAT

DON'T WORRY. JUST STAY CLOSE.
VOOON
DOMAIN EXPAN-SION!
COFFIN OF THE IRON MOUNTAIN

WHAT— ?!
WHAT IS THIS?!
DUM DUM DUM DUM
THIS IS *DOMAIN EXPANSION.*
AN ENVIRONMENT CONSTRUCTED WITH CURSED ENERGY AND MANIFESTED THROUGH A CURSED TECHNIQUE.
HOT!
THE DOMAIN YOU GUYS EXPERIENCED AT THE FACILITY WAS AN UNFINISHED ONE THAT WASN'T MANIFESTED USING A CURSED TECHNIQUE.
YOU GUYS WOULD HAVE BEEN DEAD IF IT WAS A PROPER DOMAIN.
MEGUMI PROBABLY KNEW THAT.
CONSTRUCT-ING A DOMAIN USES A TON OF CURSED ENERGY...
...BUT CAN BE WORTH IT.
HOT!
FIRST OFF, YOU GET AN UPGRADE IN STATS DUE TO THE ENVIRON-MENT.
KINDA LIKE A *BUFF* IN VIDEO GAMES.
HOT!
HOT!

ALSO...
BOOM
TCH!
THE AVERAGE JUJUTSU SORCERER WOULD HAVE BURNED UP JUST ENTERING MY DOMAIN.
CURSED TECHNIQUE DEPLOYED IN THE DOMAIN...
FWSH FWSH
...WILL ALWAYS HIT.

ALWAYS ?!
ALLLL-WAYS.
BUT NO WORRIES. THERE ARE COUNTERS.
HIT IT WITH JUJUTSU LIKE I DID.
ILLUS-TRATION: GOJO
A
B
A
A
B
I DON'T RECOMMEND THIS, BUT YOU CAN ALSO RUN AWAY.
ALMOST IMPOSSIBLE.
AND...
YOUR INFINITY! IF WE'RE HERE IN MY MORE POTENT DOMAIN...
...MY JUJUTSU WILL NOW REACH YOU, CORRECT?
BA—M
YUP.
IT SURE WILL.
INFINITY?
GIVE ME THE PRISON REALM.
I'LL ADD IT TO THE COL-LECTION!
I CAME HERE HALF SERIOUSLY.
IF I COULDN'T KILL HIM, IT WOULDN'T BE A BIG DEAL.
BUT...
...HE SHOWED ME...
...THE DIFFERENCE IN OUR POWER.

AS A CURSED SPIRIT...
...WITH THE PRIDE OF A NEW HUMAN...
I WON'T ACCEPT IT!
THE MOST EFFECTIVE COUNTER TO DOMAIN EXPANSION...
...IS TO EXPAND YOUR OWN.
FSH
WHEN MULTIPLE DOMAINS ARE EXPANDED AT THE SAME TIME, THE MORE POLISHED ONE WILL REIGN SUPREME.
IT CAN ALSO DEPEND ON COMPATIBILITY AND CURSED ENERGY.
I WON'T EVEN LEAVE A SINGLE ASH BEHIND...
...SATORU GOJO!!
DOMAIN EXPANSION.

UNLIMITED VOID!

WHAT HAPPENED? WAS MY DOMAIN SUPPRESSED?
I CAN'T SEE ANYTHING... I CAN'T FEEL ANYTHING...
NO.
I CAN SEE EVERYTHING!!
I CAN FEEL EVERYTHING!!
THE INFORMATION HAS NO END!!

AND BECAUSE OF THAT, I CAN'T DO ANYTHING!!
SHP
YOU'RE INSIDE THE LIMITLESS.
PERCEPTION. COMMUNICATION.
THE ACTIONS YOU TAKE IN LIFE ARE FORCED UPON YOU INFINITELY.
IRONIC, ISN'T IT?
GIVEN EVERYTHING, BUT UNABLE TO DO ANYTHING.
DYING SLOWLY.
I THINK I'LL STOP HERE...
...SINCE THERE ARE SOME THINGS I WANT TO ASK YOU.
VNN

SPLUCK
KRAK
THUD
THUD
SO...

WHO SENT YOU?
KRSH
HE'S THE STRONGEST JUJUTSU SORCERER!
HE'S ON A WHOLE OTHER LEVEL THAN US.
YIKES!
WHADDAYA THINK? SHOULD WE SAVE HIM?
PLP

I'D RATHER NOT WRITE ABOUT THIS!

EXPLANATION

LIMITLESS CURSED TECHNIQUE

PART 2

Continued → Next is applications for Reverse cursed technique.

• About Unlimited Void...

← In this scene, when Jogo says, "The information has no end," you might already have an idea of what that's supposed to mean, but if you were to use what he strictly sees as an example, it's...

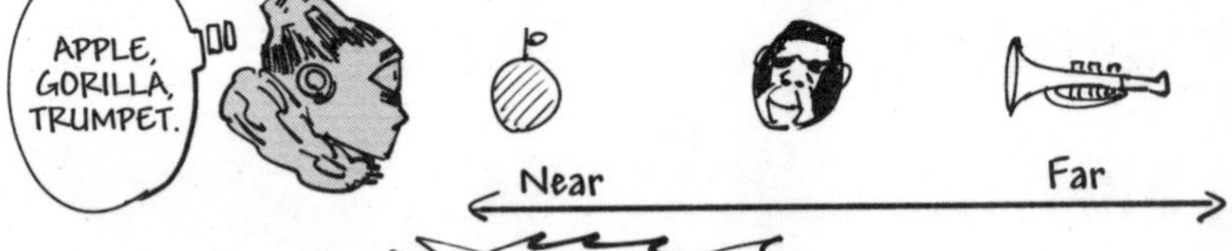

NOT THIS!!

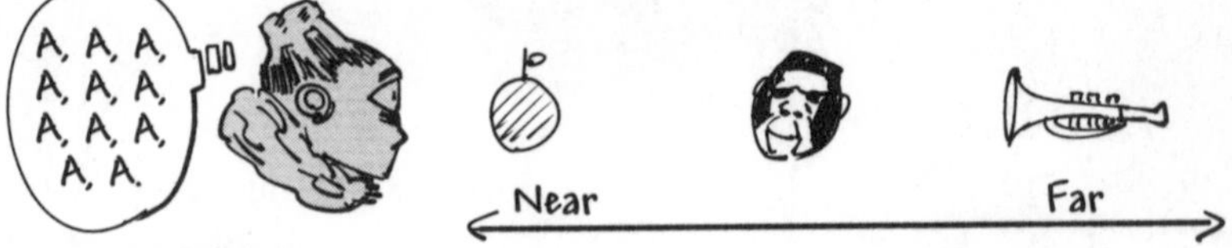

It's more like this. "I can see everything" should be, "I feel like I can see everything."

→ Continued in part 3

CHAPTER 16: AFFECTION

I CAN'T AFFORD TO BE SEEN BY ANYONE FROM THAT SCHOOL...
...SO I'LL BE GOING NOW.
IF YOU WANT TO HELP HIM, HELP HIM.
I DON'T KNOW IF YOU CURSED SPIRITS FEEL AFFECTION FOR EACH OTHER, THOUGH.
FSH
TALKING BIG.
KNOW YOUR PLACE, CURSED SPIRIT!
POOF

NOT THE TYPE TO TAKE ORDERS, HUH?
IS THERE SOMETHING NICE WAITING FOR YOU IF YOU KILL ME?
ANYWAY, WHO'RE WE LOOKING FOR?
HURRY UP! I'M GONNA EXORCISE YOU!
I'LL EXORCISE YOU EITHER WAY.
C'MON MAN! I'M GONNA KILL YA!
SO CURSES CAN TALK?
I ALMOST FORGOT ABOUT THAT.
!

THWAK
KRIK KRIK KRIK
!!

FOOSH
FLOWERS...
WHEE!
THIS IS JUJUTSU, RIGHT? I DON'T SENSE ANY KILLING INTENT.
SLAP
YIKES!
FLUNK

TMP
TMP
I'M FINE, SENSEI! GO AFTER THEM!
SWIP
WHAK
WHAK
WHAK
WAIT! KIDDING!
HELP!
GLEAM

THUD
FSH
HM.
IT GOT AWAY.
IT'S GOOD AT ERASING ITS PRESENCE.
AND IT'S A LOT MORE CREEPY THAN VOLCANO HEAD.
HIGH-LEVEL CURSED SPIRITS WORKING TOGETHER?
THIS IS GETTING FUN.
I'M VERY SORRY. IT GOT AWAY BECAUSE OF ME. BUT IT WAS YOU WHO BROUGHT ME HERE, RIGHT?
—YUJI

YUJI...
IT'S NOT JUST YOU—I WANT ALL OF YOU KIDS TO GET STRONG ENOUGH TO BEAT SOMETHING LIKE THAT.
WIN AGAINST THAT?!
THAT.
SET A GOAL AND WORK HARD TO GET THERE.
WE'RE GONNA SPEED UP THE SCHEDULE A BIT. FOR THE NEXT MONTH, YOU'RE GONNA WATCH MOVIES AND FIGHT ME.
FIGHT YOU?!
I WONDER IF I'LL BE ALIVE IN A MONTH... —YUJI
IT'S BETTER TO HAVE A SOLID GOAL, RIGHT?
GLAD I BROUGHT YA!
UM, I HAD NO IDEA WHAT WAS GOING ON.
IS THIS GUY SERIOUS?
AFTER THAT, FIELD-WORK.
I'LL HAVE YOU TAKE ON TOUGH MISSIONS.
YOU'LL LEARN THE BASICS OF JUJUTSU AND HOW TO USE IT.
WE'LL SHOW OFF YOUR RESULTS AT THE GOODWILL EVENT!
QUES-TION!
FWP
YES, YUJI?!
POINT
WHAT'S THE GOODWILL EVENT?
DIDN'T I TELL YA?

GRRRR
GAHHHH
HE'S LATE!
KLIK

KREEEAK
KLIK
THIS IS QUITE THE CALM DOMAIN.

FSSSSHHH...
FSHH...
WHAT'S HAPPENING TO JOGO, GETO?
AT DEATH'S DOOR.
BUT HANAMI WENT AFTER HIM, SO HE'S PROBABLY OKAY.
FSH
FSH

HOW IRRESPON-SIBLE. YOU ENCOURAGED HIM, RIGHT?
HARDLY. I TRIED TO STOP HIM.
SPEAK OF THE DEVIL...
KSH
JOGO. HANAMI.
I'M GLAD YOU'RE OKAY.
WHAT THE HELL ARE YOU TALKING ABOUT?!
KRR RK

YOU GOT OFF EASY.
GLARE
I THINK YOU UNDER-STAND NOW...
ABOUT SATORU GOJO AND THE RIGHT TIME AND PLACE.
WE NEED TO GET EVERY ADVANTAGE IF WE'RE TO SEAL HIM.
WE'LL PROCEED ON OCTOBER 31 IN SHIBUYA.
I'LL GIVE YOU THE DETAILS LATER.
IS THAT OKAY, MAHITO?

NO OBJECTIONS.
LET'S BE CUNNING.
WORTHY OF A *CURSE*. WORTHY OF A *HUMAN*.

KA DUNK
I WISH WE HAD MORE VENDING MACHINES...
NOT GONNA HAPPEN. WE'RE STRICT WITH WHO WE DO BUSINESS WITH.
WHUT? WHERE'S THE FIRST-YEAR CREW?
RUNNING ERRANDS.
I ♡

WILL THEY BE OKAY?
THEY'RE NOT KIDS. THEY CAN RUN ERRANDS.
THAT'S NOT WHAT I MEAN.
ISN'T THE KYOTO SCHOOL COMING TODAY?
THE MEETING FOR THE GOODWILL EVENT!
!
THERE'S TALK THAT THE HIGHER-UPS, WHO HAVE FRICTION WITH SATORU, WERE INVOLVED WITH...
...THE SPECIAL GRADE INCIDENT AND THE DISPATCH OF THE FIRST-YEARS.
THE KYOTO PRINCIPAL IS ONE OF THOSE HIGHER-UPS.
WHAT IF THEY START SOMETHING?
THEY TARGETED ITADORI, AND HE'S DEAD.
I DON'T THINK MEGUMI AND KUGISAKI ARE IN DANGER.
THE KYOTO GEEZER WOULDN'T TRY SOMETHING SO OPENLY.

THE TEACHERS HAVE THEIR REPUTATIONS.
BUT NOT THE STUDENTS.
...
IS...
...MAI COMING?
PROBABLY NOT.
THE STUDENTS AREN'T INVOLVED WITH THE MEETING.
BUT...
THOSE GUYS LOVE TO TALK TRASH.

WHY ARE YOU HERE, ZEN'IN SENPAI?
I KNEW IT! THEY HAVE A SIMILAR VIBE.
SISTERS?
OH, FUSHIGURO. ISN'T THAT WHAT YOU CALL MAKI?
CALL ME MAI.
KYOTO JUJUTSU HIGH SECOND-YEAR MAI ZEN'IN
SO THESE ARE...
...THE REPLACEMENTS FOR OKKOTSU AND THE THIRD-YEAR.
KYOTO JUJUTSU HIGH THIRD-YEAR AOI TODO
WE WERE WORRIED, SO WE TAGGED ALONG.
I HEARD YOUR CLASSMATE DIED.
MUST'VE BEEN TOUGH.

OR MAYBE IT WASN'T?
WHAT ARE YOU GETTING AT?
IT'S OKAY. SOME THINGS ARE HARD TO PUT IN WORDS.
SO I'LL DO IT FOR YOU.
"VESSEL" SOUNDS HARMLESS.
BUT HE WAS BASICALLY A HALF-CURSE MONSTER.
SUCH A VILE FACADE OF A HUMAN...
...WAS CALLING HIMSELF A JUJUTSU SORCERER ALONGSIDE YOU.
IT MUST HAVE BEEN TERRIBLE.

YOU MUST BE RELIEVED HE'S DEAD.
MAI, STOP TALKING NONSENSE.
I JUST WANT TO KNOW IF THEY'RE WORTHY REPLACEMENTS FOR OKKOTSU.
FUSHIGURO, WAS IT...?
KSH
BAM
WHAT TYPE OF GIRLS DO YOU LIKE?

?
RIP
DEPENDING ON YOUR ANSWER, I'LL BEAT YOU HALF TO DEATH.
RIP
AND I'LL DRAG OUT OKKOTSU, OR AT LEAST THE THIRD-YEAR.
RIP
BY THE WAY, I...
...LIKE TALL GIRLS...
...WITH BIG BUTTS!
TO BE CONTINUED

I'D RATHER NOT WRITE ABOUT THIS!

EXPLANATION

LIMITLESS CURSED TECHNIQUE

PART 3

• Cursed technique can also be hereditary. The Limitless cursed technique is an example. So is there anyone other than Gojo—the strongest character in the manga—who can use Limitless?! The answer is yes. However, Limitless is extremely difficult to use and requires a sophisticated manipulation of cursed energy. Even though there are other sorcerers with the possibility of using the Limitless cursed technique, Satoru Gojo is the only who can use it because he possesses a special "eye."

• Gojo is also seen teleporting in both volumes, but that can only be done under certain conditions.

*APPARENTLY MY THICK-LEGGED FEMALE CHARACTERS IN MY ONE-SHOT STORIES BECAME A LITTLE NEWSWORTHY. I ALSO HUMILIATED MYSELF A BIT IN THE AUTHOR INTRO.

*I LOOK NOTHING LIKE MY BROTHER.

MY BROTHER IS CARRYING HIS WIFE WHILE PLAYING SOCCER.
(MY BROTHER IS GOOD AT SOCCER.)
BRO
WIFE
ALL RIGHT! LET'S GO WITH THIS!
SENDAI, THE DAY BEFORE THE WEDDING...
I'M HOME!
WELCOME BACK! LOOK, GEGE! KABA-CHAN IS BACK TO LOOKING SEXY!
AMAZING!
TV
MOM
THAT'S LILICO!
DID YOU DRAW THE WELCOME BOARD?
OF COURSE!!
RUSTLE
OH, IT'S LILICO.
HERE YOU GO!

HELLO!
BRO
WIFE
KCHHK
?
WHAT'S WRONG?
SHIVER
SHIVER
HEY...H-HEY... WHAT IS THIS...?
SHIVER
I'M THE YOUNGER BROTHER...
NICE TO MEET YOU.
IT WAS THE DAY BEFORE THE WEDDING, AND I WAS OUT OF MATERIALS TO REDO THE DRAWING. I FELT TERRIBLE.
SHIVER
SHIVER
SHIVER
THERE STOOD SOMEONE WHO WAS MUCH SKINNIER THAN THE DRAWING.
WIFE
?
SKINNNNY
END
AFTER THAT INCIDENT, I REALIZED WOMEN CAN BE MUCH MORE FIT THAN I PREVIOUSLY THOUGHT, AND I REASSESSED THE WAY I DRAW THEM.
BRO
THANKS FOR DRAWING ME SO NICELY...
WIFE
KIND
KINDA CHUBBY, NO?
NOT HELPFUL

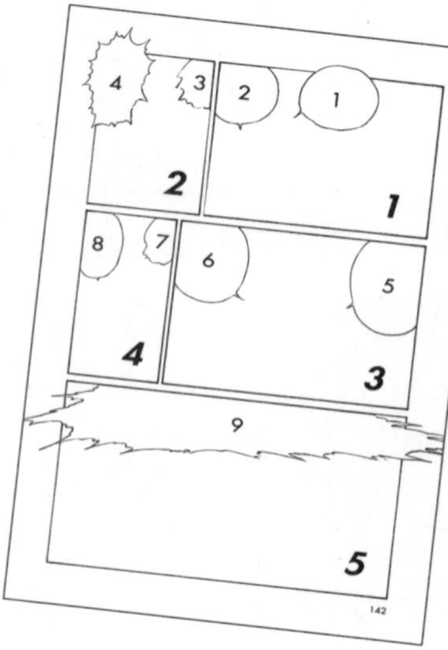

JUJUTSU KAISEN reads from right to left, starting in the upper-right corner. Japanese is read from right to left, meaning that action, sound effects and word-balloon order are completely reversed from English order.